GW00503208

Masking
Fake

M.L STORER

POEMS

MASKING FAKE

Choking on the fumes of the fire

The pyromaniacs lit up desire

Sick of pulling my teeth

Sick of holding the pliers

Can't twist them enough

To cut these puppet strings and wires.

Use my body as your spark

As the incendiaries embark

The one test that mattered

I fell short of the mark

And no flame can ever, light up all my dark.

You've become the protagonist

Taken over the role of my life

Ripped up all the pages

Detached the feelings from the spine

Taking the limelight

I can see it from behind these eyes

It's like you type these words for me

But I'm still the one who writes the lines.

I look the same

But I'm suffocating behind this mask

Designed to make it easier

But feels like I'm choking on gas

Claustrophobic in my own skin

An asphyxiated evil twin

Something inhuman

I'd give everything to surpass

You can't see the wind

Doesn't mean it ever stops blowing on the glass.

The truth is spoken

But the filter of dissociation is broken

And always finding ways to circulate

Something fake

Until I choke

And break

Like the particular particles of reality

That pass me by

It's like living and dying

To crack the sky

And get back through

To the other side.

But there's no known fail-safe

No reset or restart

So these demons inside

Continue to rip me apart.

Torn between the choice

As to swim or sink

And accept my fate of being frozen in time

At the brink

Of life & death

Or, well, whatever time I have left

And you can't tell me to take my mind off it

Cause it's like an abduction, a theft.

And I can't sleep at night

Because I'm obsessed

With the thought of waking up as me again

So I can't get to rest.

It's a feeling of true loss of self-restraint

Locked away and entombed

No matter how hard you fight

Past perceptions can't be resumed.

But you appear to function well

You must be happy…

Because that's what the others presumed.

Keep on assuming mental health isn't an issue

Our society is doomed.

INEFFABLE GAS

I hide behind my mask

But still choking

From an ineffable gas.

Depression torments you

Like a bully, it'll have the last laugh.

Why is the thought of a noose so pretty

When the outcome is so shitty?

Why am I so good at pretending to be funny and witty

When I'm a storm lurking over the city?

Dark and undesirable

The rain ruins your plans

Depression may be the slaughter

But do you really think we chose to be the lambs?

I'm stuck in oblivion, I've shouted out for help

Until I was blue in the face

But our mental health services

Are a fucking disgrace.

Everybody suddenly wants to talk

Nobody wants to do a thing

It's like declaring your love to someone

But you'll never buy them that ring.

It's an ongoing problem which I fear will never be put right

Too much demand for a service, still expected to save a life.

So many people are choking

On the fumes of negative thinking

Their hearts are sinking

And so they resort to drinking.

So where are all the older people with scars on their arms?

Did they just get better at hiding it

Or never made it this far?

Why is it not a real illness

And how is it just for attention?

Those narrow-minded fucks

Don't they deserve a mention?

Picking on you for what you wear

Or maybe you have a different sexual orientation

Let's give up

This game of fate

Just let me leave

This detached state

Then softly she said to tell them

Do not resuscitate.

Since I'm dead inside

Put down the defibrillator

Whispers from the afterlife

That she hopes to see me later

I had a way with words

But in the end

Your words

Had their way with me

Are my lungs half full, or empty?

When I drown in misery.

Just too far away

And won't reveal her true face

Cause tears roll like the tides

The moon puts into place.

INDIGO INSIDE

I'm Indigo inside

Hope's access, has been denied

Remember when I thought I could fight it off?

Still had some life left in my eyes.

The brightest lights can't shimmer through

Now that sleight of hand conceals the view

Send me some purpose

I'll send an IOU.

And I wish that there was nothing to see

I wish there was nothing that I could miss

To stop me from dying

To escape this dark abyss.

Because in hindsight

Life used to be so crystal clear

Apart from trusting too much

Believing everything I hear.

I never planned to let anyone down

But you see, this really wasn't my decision

I know you'd think differently

If you saw my latest incision.

Just a lesser of two evils

And that's the evil that won

But I did it to get through

So that you could still say you have a son.

Well, here I am outside of my own body

I don't know if and when I'll return

I wish you knew how hard I was working

Even though I do not earn.

I wish you could see me just for a day

How I see myself through my own eyes

Disconnected in a dream world

Like a dead man in disguise.

I could never let go of the things that broke me

Cause emotionally is still abuse

And Rosie, I had my head held high

To reach your pretty noose.

My self-confidence was a shipwreck

Though I floated on among debris

But this disorder is the anchor

Pulling me down below the sea.

My soul burns away, like gas in a blaze

And it hurts to hear that positive thinking

Will help to tame the brain.

Of course it would, but that's like the limb that's missing

Along with my personality

How do I simply do these things

With a fucked up functionality?

It's like a ghost at night

That you have to see to believe

And just because someone showed a smile

Doesn't mean the demons can

So quickly up and leave.

Always there in the shadows

Loitering in the night

And just because I feed it these pills

Doesn't mean it never bites.

TRIPWIRE

Dark skies rise inside

Covered by little white lies

Like "honestly I'm fine"

On death row just doing my time

Taking the punishment

Though I didn't do the crime.

Emotionally abused

Scavenged and used

My head is just a ticking time bomb

Impossible to be defused

It's no tempest in a teapot

When depression's been infused

And a strainer on standby

For when your old self gets removed.

Just a shell

A skeleton, shackled in chains

And tripwires to safeguard

Escapees in the brain.

They're all bad to the bone

But they've made themselves at home

Because my negativity feeds them

In these sick seeds I have sown.

Cutting the right wires is the only hope that remains,
until you remember the green and blue tubes running with
red are your veins.

Too much havoc

Triggered trip wires

Alternate reality

Self-control's not required.

I feel like a phantom

Floating like fumes above the west coast

But close to going south, like words thrown from my mouth

I'm burning in the fire but can't leave the house.

Etched among flashbacks, carved is your name

Like a beautiful beast branded

I've no control to ever tame.

With no remorse

It's my head that she stalks

But still, this pain will remain locked away

Alongside the bad thoughts

But she can escape

She contorts.

Daunting like a ghost

But it's no home that she haunts.

SONAR

Black tinted glass

Embroils a new disguise

A chamber of secrets

Behind sockets of sad eyes.

Out of his depth

In diving pools of tears

Lost in nitrogen narcosis

Segments of his soul disappear.

A day of the dead

In memory of these last few years

But sadly I'm not the only one

And we're no pioneers.

My flair has gone

Burnt out like a candle

Trying to write in the dark

Like a blindfolded vandal.

What's life

With a perforated perception?

And telling myself

I'm the definition of deception.

I'm just a double-edged sword

My hands are too sore to grip

Depersonalization is the torpedo

That will sink this battleship.

Reality echoes away like sonar

I never thought you'd take it so far

A twisted alteration of the mind

Like wreckage, you won't find

This is trauma and terror's love child

With toxic teeth intertwined

And if I maintain drowning in silence

I'm sure you won't mind.

Like a lunatic on the lunar surface

Versus a service falling out of orbit

Who could plan it…

Perhaps the politics of a bloodshed coloured palette?

Running rings around savings

Observing Uranus

Still not as cold as the dead

Who struggled to be so tenacious.

Crawling night skies of acid rain

No star dust shines enough

To cloak all the pain

Just a masterful disguise

A smile to scrutinize

When a little light seeps through

The cracks in the clouds

Like rain, sometimes it's torrential, sometimes it's in bouts

These things don't demand opinions

No need to cast your doubts.

Submerged

In an abode aquatic

Dramatic.

Gasping for air like an asthmatic

The others take oxygen for granted

It makes you frantic

You're left stranded but you roll with the punches

Hindered like a one-armed bandit

Still more fruitful than the hope you clung on to

The will to live your demons demanded

This machine is broken

Still, you feed it everything you've got

Three apples roll down

But they're beginning to rot

There's an evil empress in the mechanism

Wallowing within a witchcraft exorcism

To bring back

Bad memories from the dead

Hell-bent

With a price on your head

But don't they know that place is a minefield?

Better be careful where they tread.

FOOT ON A LAND MINE

Life is like a wasteland

Scattered with mines below the ground.

We all take different paths

To succeed and do the best we can

But one accidental route you take, and *click*

You hear that sound.

Maybe you had a hard childhood, a bad relationship,
suffered from abuse or problems with drink/drugs.

Perhaps something else entirely

Or maybe you don't even know what started this.

A switch has tripped and you're frozen in time

You can't move forward with your life

And you struggle to recall what was behind.

You often hear people say "Think positively"

Or "Try to take your mind off of it"

But regardless of their bad advice, you're still in the shit.

They can't see the mental state we are in

Like the brain shutting down, an inch away from death

And you beg for someone to understand

Only under your breath.

It's like your foot is on a land mine

Stuck in a terrifying state

You question everything you've done

Mistake after mistake

My hands aren't mine

My reflection scares me

And the memories feel so fake

Everything in my life appears truly opaque.

Half of you is torn between just stepping off

And removing the pressure

The other half, desperate to get back on the path

Because you want to get better.

How do you begin to explain what goes through your mind

When you heard that click?

When the switch in your brain tripped

And your emotions and memories were stripped.

Words escape my mouth

Before I even think of what to say

And no decision

Is as clear as night and day

I want to feel normal

Before I forget what it was like

You feel absolutely crazy

When you explain to your psych

About this unknown disorder

With a harsh grip on your life

That you test reality

With things as sharp as a knife

My life feels like a film

That no one wants to view

Recovery is always too late

For the rendezvous.

Until it arrives

I'll be waiting with one foot on a mine

The other anxiously tapping

In the hope

I'll be saved in time.

VANTABLACK

My very soul is just a light trap

Shying away from the entrance

To that realm of happiness

This mind is more than dark

Serotonin lies in the shadows

Stealthily attacked

My past self awaits the oblivion within

I'm merely a shadow

No depth

No way to cut myself some slack

I can't see myself in the crystal clear definition I used to

I'm more than dark.

I'm Vantablack.

I can't emit what little light I have left

Although it's too slight to be seen

Like a pilot light flickering in a basement

Deep blue in colour

But burning over a thousand degrees

Squandering the little energy

I have left to spare

On the few reasons I can salvage

Of why I still care

Spiralling out of control

Like a whirlpool in the sea

That's two pairs of brimful lungs

Reserved for you and me

Why do we have to wait so long for help?

As if we aren't subjected to this impending doom

I've 'lived' three years of my life

Confined to this claustrophobic cocoon

Like a transparent safety blanket that no one else can see

Particularly the inward pointing needles

Sucking the life from out of me

Family seem to care about your well being

But sometimes, not as much as getting employed

As if a few months at rest is a 'laziness' you've enjoyed

And that in absence of help

You magically filled in the void.

Can you really put a price on your mental health?

Is it worth less than earning money week to week?

Well now for me

The value of my life

Is a currency obsolete.

You can assume somebody is alive

Without hearing their heartbeat

But is it fair to assume the 'feeling'

When their expectations ride shotgun

With your needs slumped over the backseat?

There is no sound for the plummet of self-worth

Especially from the summit of condescension

They've been constructing since birth.

So load another shell

To your barrel of laughs

In your delusional perfect earth

And step on the gas

Oblivious to the mental minefield

Where the wretched ones

Walk among glass.

FRAGMENTATION

Like the Flying Dutchman

Anchored to the locker of Davy Jones

This phantasm of reality

Is sinking like stones

Can't feel my own presence

Can't feel it in my bones

I feel like a shadow

Concealing dark undertones.

Like a ship in the night

Pushed overboard

They hope you're incised

Cause the deeper you sink; the sharks are harder to fight

I guess that's what you could call an underbite.

Stripped of control

After twenty-two years of existence

You try everything possible to stop

But keep on going the distance

Branded by demons, in the form of red scars upon the skin

Like a tally keeping count, on their odds to win.

It seems that if nothing is physical, nobody bats an eyelid.
No need for hands over eyes, they're already so blinded.

I just hit the nail on the head

So many humans

So judgemental on issues

So damn widespread

And it hurts just that little bit more

Coming from a hand that fed.

A pencil in a vice

Led to sacrifice

Half ready to snap

Used to etch their designs

To fortify the most stigmatizing trap

If depression is black, this needs a darker shade.
To portray despair as existence begins to fade.

A puppet to an entity, where the ropes are far from frayed

It's a pressurizing battle, taking everything to maintain

One hand reaching for the pin

The other grasping a grenade.

The frightful fragmentation

The shrapnel p a r a d e s

Shellshock and suffering

Turn these ripples to cascades.

PRONE TO PROVOKE

Like the strike of a viper

You just cannot dodge

No antivenom

Only antidepressants

To restrain

And dislodge

These deeply ingrained thoughts

And reckless ruminations

But the drugs only add to

The lack of her sensations

Just like tentacles

Dancing in black ink

A mechanism blinding perceptions

Since being pushed to the brink

The way our minds work

It's just an act of propulsion

She gets propelled to new lows

And crash lands in compulsion

A corrupted mind once fluorescent

Now shrouded in darkness

These destructive new ways

Become too heavy to harness.

She distorted old memories

In to deep crevices within

As unreal as her whole being

Wrapped in unacquainted skin.

Talking about it

Always seems to get sidestepped

Because the shoulder she used to lean on

Rests the head of an illiterate mindset

Sometimes it's best to keep things to herself

Away from the others

Cause they've grown prone to provoke

And add fuel to her fire

Triggering billowing black smoke

They say it's her in control of her issues

As if it's all some big joke

So next time she holds her breath

Because she'd rather not choke

It's like explaining music to the deaf

And vision to the blind

But because it's not physical

Pleads for help are outshined

She would rather be bleeding

Or show signs of disease

Cause then everyone shows compassion

Cause we've all fell and scraped our knees.

We've all had a headache

They've likely faced a loss

So why do they frown upon the cuts

On her arm

That go up and across?

Yes, it's all in her head

But it came from her heart

At least she won't suffer for life

Like you

With your head up your arse.

THE CONSTANT

People are the constant

That lead others to despondence

So tell me, right now

How clean is your conscience?

Oscillating to the rhythm

Of heartbroken precision

Bandoliers of bullets

Can't touch this apparition

This prowling poltergeist

Isn't so easy to entice

Like a dead man's hand

Just can't roll the dice.

The devil rages inside me and you

Stuck to unreality like glue

Like a broken record spinning

Déjà entendu.

And you think

Why do we have to wait so long for help?

Just because it's all in our head

It's a dark killer, taken too lightly

Because it's too late when you're dead.

Like a gunshot to the head

Once it was only a thought

Because they still had some hope

Maybe that young girl who enjoyed skipping with her friends

Got left out

So she found a new use for that rope

And they'll all say the signs weren't clear enough

To be put under the microscope.

Quick to find a loophole,

To justify a delayed solution

As long as you can sleep at night

With your new found absolution.

RETROGRADE

I'm just a satellite

Lost within space

An interstellar stowaway

Disguised deep inside my brain

Locked in rusty chains

Away from asteroid rain

She's the trespasser of

Once unscathed domains.

It feels like my brains in retrograde

By maintaining this masquerade

A parallax parade

Patronizingly portrayed.

Like a mind engulfed

In waves of gamma rays

Isolated and helpless

I'm an astronaut ablaze

Sinking in a deep blue like Neptune

A maelstrom in a monsoon.

Dragooned by my demons

A sinister scheme

Forced upon me too soon

You were my cerulean constellation

Now you're just damnation

Where the oxygen's on

The brink of desolation

Abandon all hope

It's primed for detonation.

ULTRAVIOLET

Ever contrasting is this life

It's violence

Under ultraviolet lights

And little victories

In the black of night

Sometimes it's just a bitch though

Be careful, she bites.

Turquoise tears

Of tragedy and turmoil

Vermilion blood

Brought up to a boil

Just a restless resident

Inside this machine

Running inside veins

Of aquamarine

Tangled in a mind

Between a nightmare and a dream

Packed with envy

Like a malachite green

Of those not blindsided

By a life without means

There's nothing I can see

That isn't what it seems.

A life consumed by mist

Our demons insist

That this harrowing haze

Makes it easier

To cope and coexist

But I can't connect to reality

The transmissions been bewitched

Like a boy with a stitch that persists

And twists like a knife

Devoid of intermission

So here goes, my final disquisition.

On this Houdini within

So eloquently persistent

Passing the current

So I can't handle the resistance.

Trapped in the vicinity of a vortex

In my prefrontal cortex

This mind is no home

So I sleep on the doorstep

I kicked myself out

There's only vacancies to vanquish

Any other feelings

Except for my anguish.

Everybody leads you to pain

In some way or another

Even yourself

Except you're undercover

Disguised within

To bring-forth flashes of an old lover

And here's me thinking

The pills could clean up the clutter.

This life is just fragments of a mess

And we were born to confess

These defences we built

We either undress or suppress

So my demons and I digress

Cause there's no better way to waste my breath

Than to describe and help others

Trapped inside this disorder like death.

Like a catacomb of confusion I caress

Though I'm always in its debt

Casting a shadow over me

Like a sedentary silhouette

The past paints a picture of regret

No reset or restart.

Just like love

This will tear us apart.

Printed in Poland
by Amazon Fulfillment
Poland Sp. z o.o., Wrocław